the seeds of love

First published in Great Britain in 1990 by
Virgin Books
26 Grand Union Centre
338 Ladbroke Grove
London, W10 5AH

Text by Adrian Thrills: copyright © Virgin Music (Publishers) Ltd. 1990. Words and music by Roland Orzabal and Nicky Holland: copyright © Virgin Music (Publishers) Ltd. / 10 Music Ltd. 1989, except 'Woman in Chains' and 'Standing On the Corner of the Third World': words and music by Roland Orzabal: copyright © Virgin Music (Publishers) Ltd. 1989, and 'Sowing the Seeds of Love': words and music by Roland Orzabal and Curt Smith: copyright © Virgin Music (Publishers) Ltd. 1989.

Cataloguing in Publication Data is available on request from the British Library

Design by Stylorouge
Set in Garamond ITC Italic, Franklin Gothic ITC (italic / roman / bold)
by T.P.P. Limited
Photography David Scheinman / Avid Images *(cover and pages 1, 2, 5, 8, 9, 12, 14, 17, 20, 21, 22, 24, 30, 34, 35, 37, 40, 45, 46, 48, 49, 50, 52, 53, 56, 64)*
Simon Fowler *(pages 28, 48, 49, 59, 60, 61, 62, 63)*

Printed and bound in Great Britain by
Butler & Tanner Ltd, Frome and London

It all started on a summer evening in 1985. In the lounge of the Hyatt Regency Hotel in Kansas City, a group of English musicians were relaxing after a sell-out show in one of the town's larger auditoria.

Tears For Fears were midway through a demanding North American tour promoting their multi-million-selling *Songs From The Big Chair* album. The record had already spawned two US No.1 singles in 'Shout' and 'Everybody Wants To Rule The World' and the accompanying roadshow was proving to be one of the hottest tickets on that year's concert merry-go-round.

It should have been a cause for some celebration. But, in the hotel bar, emotions were mixed and the mood strangely subdued. A vital spark had been missing from that night's show. It had been the same the night before. And the night before that...

As the day hit the night, the elegant brown frame of the hotel's resident entertainer took her usual place behind a white baby grand piano. Accompanied only by the barely audible jazz shuffle of a brushed drum and an upright bass, Oleta Adams sat by candlelight and began to play. Her voice floated out above the muffled chatter and into the pervading emptiness of the hotel bar.

For Roland Orzabal and Curt Smith, listening to Oleta was a relevation. Here was a musical performance that was raw and honest, pure and soulful. In contrast with their own show, with its backing tapes, lighting rigs, marathon soundchecks and business-like emphasis on perfection, this was music with only the most basic embellishment. The impact on Roland and Curt was deep and lasting: this chance encounter with Oleta Adams was to prove a watershed in the career of Tears For Fears.

For Roland Orzabal and Curt Smith, listening to Oleta was a revelation. Here was a musical performance that was raw and honest, pure and soulful.

Four years on from that night in Kansas City, Roland Orzabal is sitting in the front room of his North London home. He is surrounded by the material fruits of his success. The trappings, however, are not those of the run-of-the-mill pop personality. There are a couple of original pieces of Abstract Expressionism, a word processor and shelf after shelf of astrological, scientific and social literature. This man is obviously an avid reader.

He is also an earnest and engaging talker. And every time he recalls that first encounter with Oleta, he sees a slightly different perspective on its precise relevance. He starts to explain:

'Coming across Oleta was a reminder of the power of music. It was a reminder of what music could do, a reminder that music should basically be about self-expression. It was an emotional experience for me.

'At that time, we were acting out the roles of successful players in the music business. Running into Oleta showed us the other side of the coin. It brought us face-to-face with music on a pure level. Here was someone literally singing for her supper but still expressing herself brilliantly. Oleta's roots were in blues and gospel, but she had been told to tone those aspects down and sing in a more cabaret-orientated style. Within those restrictions, however, she was still able to express herself far more honestly than we were.

'The whole performance was very immediate, very live and very personal. It wasn't passing through any medium. It was sung straight from the soul. It was also something that we had discovered for ourselves rather than something that had been sold to us by the record company. It wasn't removed or distant in the way that our own music was.'

Curt Smith shares his partner's feelings about the night in Kansas City and its profound effect on Tears For Fears.

'Seeing Oleta was a big turning point. There we were with a seven-piece band and an audience of thousands every night and yet there was no soul in what we were doing. And then there was this woman with just a piano who could reduce an audience to tears. It was amazing to see someone express themselves so naturally.'

Roland takes up the tale once more:

'Tears For Fears had been travelling across America playing songs that worked in the studio but not on the stage.

'The material was not particularly loose or free or expressive. We would have liked to be more expressive, but the songs we played were repressing those desires. Because of our backing tapes and our sequencers, we were tied to the structure of the songs.

'Most bands start making music in order to express themselves, but get waylaid in the process, particularly as they become more successful. People become diverted and get preoccupied by their niche in the marketplace. As competitive concerns become more important, self-expression tends to take a back seat.'

Roland and Curt knew they had encountered something special that night in Kansas City – both on the stage and also within themselves. They were too shellshocked by the performance they had witnessed to introduce themselves to Oleta there and then, but she would re-enter their story at a later date. The important thing at the time was that Tears For Fears rediscovered the reason why they began making music in the first place.

Returning to England in 1986 after the *Big Chair* tour, Tears For Fears took a few months off, Roland in London and Curt in their original home town of Bath in the West Country. It was a time for reflection before the commencement of work on their next project – the difficult third album.

The band had been working more or less non-stop for the previous five years. Signed to Phonogram Records by maverick A&R director David Bates in 1981, their early singles – 'Suffer The Children', 'Pale Shelter', 'Mad World' and 'Change' – were precious, introspective affairs that earned the band a rather gloomy reputation, something only increased in March 1983 by their debut album *The Hurting*. Like the band name itself, the album's thematic roots lay in psychologist Arthur Janov's controversial primal scream theory, an analysis of problems that involves the shedding of neurosis (fears) through expressing emotions (tears). Not exactly the typical concerns of your average fun-loving pop group.

Album No.2, *Songs From The Big Chair*, was released in 1985 and proved a tougher, more mature collection of songs. Produced by Chris Hughes and recorded with a band that comprised Roland and Curt with keyboard player Ian Stanley and drummer Manny Elias, it was certainly more confident and outward-looking than their debut.

Says Curt:

'The second album was definitely a growth from the first. To be honest, it was a blatant attempt at making a commercial record, even to the extent of using obvious musical devices like rockist guitar solos. It was quite disgusting. But it worked.

'The other notable thing about the second album was that we were older. As you get older, you learn to express yourself slightly better. We wanted to be amusing as well as serious, so that people could see that we weren't two dour, depressed individuals. I think that album achieved that for us.'

It was also a remarkable commercial success, selling a staggering eight million copies worldwide, half of them in America. But success brought its own attendant set of problems, from an exhausting tour schedule to the artistic frustration of a live show that was hamstrung by its own computer-programmed rigidity. The limitations of the latter had been put into sharp relief that night in Kansas City when the Tears roadshow ran headlong into the unfettered soul swing of Oleta Adams.

Both Roland and Curt knew that things had to be different on their next album. But if such a change was to be a fundamental one, it would not happen overnight. Like producer Chris Hughes and keyboard maestro Ian Stanley — credited as co-writer of half of the songs on *Big Chair* — the Tears For Fears duo were children of the electronic age.

'Having R&B music thrust at us for three or four months, culminating in the encounter with Oleta, was bound to have an effect.'

Roland and Curt might have played guitar and bass when on-stage and in the recording studio, but their music was essentially rooted in the solid rock of programmed machines. The songs on *Big Chair* and *The Hurting* had been founded on the Fairlight and strained through a sequencer.

If Tears were to change to a looser and more organic way of working, they were going to have to sacrifice some of the computerised tools of their trade. Escaping from what had become something of a musical straitjacket was to prove a painful process, as Curt explains:

'As a band, we came from the programmed pop era of the early eighties and we had inherited a sense of structure that permeated almost all our music. The way we were working was becoming too sterile. We wanted to do something more colourful, something that sounded big and warm. You cannot get that from machines. You only get that with real musicians and real players.'

The music the band had been listening to while travelling across the States on tour also had a profound impact. Specialist R&B radio stations pumping forth hour after hour of brilliant black dance music opened up totally new sonic vistas for the duo, virtually guaranteeing that their third album would lean far more heavily on soul styles. Roland admits readily to the influences:

'Having R&B music thrust at us for three or four months, culminating in the encounter with Oleta, was bound to have an effect. As music, it had such great emotional impact that it forced us to re-examine our own attitudes. It was obvious that we were trying to make emotional music within too rigid a format. Hopping across into the realm of soul and borrowing something from that made it easier to be expressive. It made our music more expressive.

'I didn't see the success of *Songs From The Big Chair* as some sort of green light. After two No.1 singles in America, we appeared to have hit on a formula that could have brought us continued success. There was obviously pressure from within the unit to continue as we were and produce 'More Songs From The Big Chair', but it wasn't what Curt and I wanted.

'There would have to be a death before we could be reborn.'

The seeds had been sown. It would take a further four years before they flowered.

part two

Recording sessions for the follow-up to *Songs From The Big Chair* began at the end of 1986. As the album took shape over what was to prove a sometimes agonising, occasionally euphoric three-year period, the working title went through almost as many changes as the band did producers and studios.

Among some of the more unwieldy monikers were such evocative mouthfuls as 'Raoul And The Kings Of Spain' (Raoul being Orzabal's oft-quoted nickname), 'Zen And The Kings Of Bohemia' (a restaurant and pub respectively in North London), 'Alight Here For Gospel Oak' (a bus-stop sign in the same vicinity) and 'Sowing The Seeds Of Love' (the eventual winner in slightly shortened form).

As was to be expected, the momentous change in direction that the Tears were seeking proved to be an expensive and time-consuming business. First pair into the producers' seats were Clive Langer and Alan Winstanley, a well-respected team responsible for some of the finest moments in the musical careers of Madness, Elvis Costello, Kevin Rowland, Robert Wyatt and Teardrop Explodes. These initial sessions, ultimately unsuccessful, ran into the early months of 1987 before the resulting tapes were binned.

A longer series of recordings, this time with the old guard of Chris Hughes and Ian Stanley, took the band up to the end of 1987, but the fruits were again rejected. The old chestnut 'musical differences' was, for once, a genuine reason; there was fundamental disagreement over the band's direction, many of the arguments stemming from the over-use of machines and programmes.

A brave move followed. With the tentative agreement of the record company – now the reactivated Phonogram offshoot label, Fontana – the band decided to produce themselves. Roland, who had declared himself 'unproduceable' after the difficulties with Chris Hughes, was to work in conjunction with engineer Dave Bascombe. First, however, he had to finish writing the songs and begin to choose a select band of musicians.

For songwriting, he turned for help to a new partner in Nicky Holland, a one-time Ravishing Beauty and former musical director of The Fun Boy Three. Nicky had provided keyboards on the arduous worldwide tour promoting the *Big Chair* album and was already well tuned-in to both Orzabal's fastidious, perfectionist nature and his designs for a more soulful, expressive Tears For Fears. Of the songs that eventually made it to the finished album, Holland worked with Orzabal on 'Badman's Song', 'Advice For The Young At Heart', 'Swords And Knives', 'Year Of The Knife' and 'Famous Last Words'. The collaboration brought about a significant shift in Roland's approach to songwriting:

'It was vital for me to work with Nicky. On "Advice" for instance, I had a set of words and then worked with her on the musical ideas. Prior to that, I had been writing on the machines with Chris and Ian, but the songs were not working out very well. Nicky's approach was more fluid.

'The fact that Nicky is a keyboard player has also added a new dimension to our writing. She took me into the realm of the piano and I learnt a lot from that. I used to write on the guitar and the synthesiser, but she got me away from that.'

'You can play more interesting and developed chords on a piano. As it says on the sleeve of the album, "thanks to Nicky for her harmonic inversions". Her knowledge of chords is far more developed than mine.'

Nicky and Roland had already collaborated on one Tears For Fears arrangement before the Seeds project — an interpretation of Robert Wyatt's 'Sea Song' that graced the B-Side of the 'I Believe' single. And, in retrospect, Holland views that collaboration as yet another pivotal point in the progression of ideas and incidents that led the Tears team to The Seeds Of Love.

'Although the Wyatt song was obviously a cover and thus involved no composition or writing, we did our own arrangement of it. The whole thing came together in a day and we both loved the way it turned out. The fact that Robert Wyatt later said in an interview that he liked it also meant a lot to us. The song was an indication that Roland and I could work together. With hindsight, it was something of a turning point.'

Nicky, sharing some of Roland's frustrations with the direction of Tears For Fears on the Big Chair tour, was also keen to work in a looser, more organic manner on the new songs.

'The gigs we were doing at the time were all very similar. The structure was very rigid and the music was consequently boring to play. The tour was nine months long and that certainly had an affect on the playing. It was impossible to change the tempo of any of the songs and even Roland initially frowned on anyone who deviated from the set pattern. The first few times I broke away from it, I would get a look from Roland that indicated it was not the done thing.

'When it came to writing, we would record things very roughly onto a cassette recorder. We would both be singing and playing at the same time, me on a piano and Roland on a guitar. We tried not to control things too much at the early stage. We wanted to let the songs evolve. My involvement was very much musical, but we would also discuss the lyrical ideas while we were putting the musical side together. On some songs, I would come up with lines or ideas, but the great bulk of the lyrical ideas were Roland's.'

Most bands start making music in order to express themselves, but get waylaid in the process, particularly as they become more successful.

As for the recording sessions, Roland gathered together a wonderfully varied posse of top sessioneers based round a hard core of drummer Manu Katche, bassist Pino Palladino, percussionist Carole Steele, guitarist Neil Taylor and – the jewel in the crown – pianist and vocalist Oleta Adams.

Over two years had elapsed since the band witnessed Oleta's breath-taking performance in the lounge of the Hyatt Regency, but she had never been far from their thoughts. It was time to invite her into the fold. Roland and Curt flew to Kansas and tracked the singer down to another hotel lounge, The Almeda, where she was still working with her trio, still singing and playing with apparently effortless simplicity and beauty. Oleta takes up the story herself: 'I don't actually remember the first time Tears For Fears came into the town. I didn't meet them personally until two years later. I remember seeing them in the audience and thinking that they looked out of place. I was pretty surprised when they came and introduced themselves, particularly when they told me that they had come over from England specifically to hear me play!

'Anyway, we spent the next three days together talking about the philosophy of music and performance and I agreed to come over and work with them on some songs. I had been promised many opportunities before, but this seemed like a chance to do things on my own terms and be taken seriously for the first time.

'The most blessed thing was that I ended up with musicians who accepted me for what I was. It was a wonderful union. As a producer, Roland also knew how to bring out the best in my performance.'

A fixture on the Kansas City music scene for over a decade, Oleta Adams had certainly paid her dues and the solo recording contract with Fontana that followed her Tears For Fears engagement was well overdue. Like many great black American female vocalists – Aretha Franklin is one very obvious example – her first musical experience had been in church.

The daughter of a Baptist preacher in Yakima, Washington, she had sung in the choir from the age of five and played the piano from the age of nine. Her first club and hotel engagements came locally in Washington before she moved halfway across the States to Kansas. She can now look back fondly on her evenings entertaining the hotel guests of Middle America:

'People were always telling me that it was impossible to have a concert situation in the bar of a hotel, but I didn't agree. For me, it was a great opportunity, my own little Broadway.

'It was great to be able to take people on a musical and emotional trip, so that the audience was buzzing by the end of the evening. People would feel good about themselves and want to behave beautifully towards other people. The next day they would go about their business with new energy. It was therapy for the people in the audience'.

Oleta features prominently on three of the key songs on *Seeds Of Love*. The opening 'Woman In Chains' is sung as a duet with Roland, while her jazzy piano is the driving force behind 'Badman's Song' as well as providing a more sedate embellishment to 'Standing On The Corner Of The Third World'. The songs were recorded as a series of live takes, sometimes even as jam sessions, by Orzabal and Bascombe, with the best sections of each take then digitally spliced together in a painstaking piece of studio engineering. But, as Curt recalls, it was not technical excellence but emotional expression that was used to gauge the suitability of a take.

'In recording the album, we were always looking for performances rather than perfection. We would sometimes record up to fifteen performances of a track before putting together the best segments to give us the complete song. It became a fine art, but the end result justified the means.'

The recording, mixing and jigsaw-style editing of *Seeds* took Roland, Curt and Dave Bascombe from the start of 1988 well into the summer of 1989, the final mix being put to bed at Mayfair Studio in North London on 15 July. For the band, working hour was now over and the perpetual perfectionists could almost allow themselves a smile.

The album was 'cut' – the master tapes processed and lacquers made up to press the vinyl – by New York cutting engineer Bob Ludwig a few days after the final mix was completed. For Dave Bascombe, initially employed as an engineer on *Songs From The Big Chair* and then again on the Chris Hughes sessions for *Seeds*, it marked the culmination of almost two years in the studio.

'When I first got involved, I thought it could be a long-running project, but I didn't realise quite how long it would run. One of the main reasons for the length of time it took was Roland's determination to capture exactly the right feel for each track. He would have a particular sound and feeling in his head, and we would try all the available routes until we eventually captured that feeling. We would record a variety of performances on digital tape, preserving something that was very spontaneous, and then use the best parts of each take to build up the complete picture.

'Some tracks changed almost beyond recognition during the recording process, such as "Badman's Song." Others are almost the same as the original demos. Some songs went through various different mixes. As something like that goes along, it gradually becomes obvious what the basic ingredients of a good mix are. With the title track, we tried a number of different things and eventually settled on our original mix.

'The change from the previous album is not just down to our attitude to working with machines: the importance of that is sometimes over-played when people talk about the record. There are a lot of machines used on the record. The change is rather down to trying to get more of a soulful feeling all round. We did use a lot more live playing than in the past, letting more people come into the frame and using what they had to offer as musicians.'

The Seeds Of Love was shipped out to record shops by Fontana in September 1989, topping the British album charts in the week of release and priming the public for another massive Tears For Fears tour in the early months of 1990. By the time the band took to the road, 'Sowing The Seeds Of Love', 'Woman In Chains' and 'Advice For The Young At Heart' had all provided Top Forty singles.

Just as its mentor had promised, the album marked the 'death' of the old, monochrome Tears sound and the dawning of a new technicolour vision that was indeed far more soulful and alive than anything the band had produced before. Musically, it was larger and more expansive, revealing a depth and diversity that swept from the ornate Beatlisms of the title track and the raunchy directness of 'Year Of The Knife' to the more reflective pastures of 'Swords And Knives' and the closing 'Famous Last Words'.

The spirit of adventure that permeated the music was echoed strongly in the songwords, many of which are explained in greater detail in this book. Drawing numerous parallels between personal conflict and wider social and political issues — the inner and the outer — the composer remained true to the psychological concerns of the first two albums, but the context was now more global and far more aware. *The Seeds Of Love* might not be the perfect *pop* album — even the band would admit as much — but it stands as perfect proof of one thing: three albums old, Tears For Fears had grown up.

The Seeds Of Love was shipped out to record shops by Fontana in September, topping the British album charts in the week of release.

Roland thinks deeply about his general feelings on the *Seeds* collection. With the benefit of a few months' hindsight, he still retains great affection for the record. He is, however, already looking tentatively forward to The Next Phase.

'It was the first album where I have been totally emphatic about what I was doing, even to the point of giving up on ideas halfway through because they weren't working. There was a lot of experimentation, a lot of shooting off on tangents. We were given the time, so we tried things we'd never tried before.

'The songs that give me the most pleasure are probably 'Woman In Chains' and 'Badman's Song'. Those are complete pieces of music. They really get there. As for the other songs, some of them are too culture-based, too era-based, to be truly timeless. The next album will take the ideas and themes of *Seeds* up a level and let them evolve.

'Now that that ideas have been set in stone, so to speak, we can refine them. Where we have been sloshing about on the canvas, we will in future become more artistic.

'As for the commercial side. I have never thought that selling a lot of records gives you real gratification. You cannot quantify artistic success like that. The greatest satisfaction comes when other people use your record as a vehicle for their own development, for their own understanding of certain feelings.

'But, having said that, I don't claim to be any kind of guru. I wouldn't want to take any credit for the feelings and emotions expressed in the songs. If this album has any particular resonance for the listener, it is simply because certain feelings have come through me. It doesn't make me a person with any special insight.

'This is a personal struggle for me. It is something that I simply have to do. In certain respects, I would love to get to the point where I don't have to do it. At the moment, though, I still feel an incredible compulsion.'

'In every man there is a woman and in every woman there is a man. I really believe in that. The feminine traits are passive rather than active.'

Roland: 'My understanding of "Woman In Chains" has changed a lot since I wrote it. A lot of people have put it down merely as a pro-feminist song, but it is not quite as simple as that. It is not just about a man repressing a woman. It is about the repression of the feminine spirit in men as much as in women.

'In every man there is a woman and in every woman there is a man. I really believe in that. The feminine traits are passive rather than active. They are receptive and inner-directed. The feminine represents the emotions and intuition, an open rather than a closed mind, and a lot of those traits are very repressed in Western society. They are chained up in both women and men. So when I sing "free her" in the song, what I am really saying is "free me".

'We live in a very lop-sided society in that respect. It is extremely patriarchal. Traditional masculine virtues and aggressive values are very much on top. Feminine virtues, on the other hand, are suppressed and often relegated to the subconscious. There is no equilibrium and that is a very dangerous thing. There are other value systems, however, outside the traditional Western ones. There are societies, often only small tribes, that are matricentric, with women at their centre. One of the most notable things about these non-patriarchal societies is that there is very little greed or violence. The whole system of values is very different from ours.'

Oleta: 'I think that "Woman In Chains" contains some of the best singing I've ever done. But talk about perfectionism! There were times during the recording when I felt like a Fairlight computer! Roland's attention to detail is amazing, running as far as getting just the right emphasis on the letter "p" in the word "hope".

'We played around with a lot of different words and verses before we settled on the version that is on the album. Roland was writing and re-writing that song right up to the last minute before it was recorded.'

woman in chains

words and music by Orzabal

Well it's a world gone cra-zy keeps wo-man in chains. ____
know what I mean

Wo-man in chains, ____ wo-man in chains. ____

Bridge
Men of stone. Men of stone. Well I feel

CODA
it's un-der my skin ____ but out of my hands ____ I'll tear it a-part ____ but I

won't un-der-stand, ____ I will not ac-cept ____ the great-ness of man ____
It's a world gone cra-zy keeps

wo-man in chains, ____ gone cra-zy keeps wo-man in chains. ____

So free ____ her, ____ so free ____ her, ____ so free ____ her, ____ so

'The song is really about guilt and remorse. There is a lot of Catholic imagery in it, a lot of Biblical references about faith moving mountains and fire quenching the soul.'

Roland: 'The song is really about guilt and remorse. There is a lot of Catholic imagery in it, a lot of Biblical references about faith moving mountains and fire quenching the soul. The images are used very much on a psychological level. The idea is that some form of punishment will lead to redemption. It all ties in very well with the gospel arrangement of the song. It was one of the tracks that Oleta could really enhance. It was a song that needed to be really authentic and it basically came together as a jam with Oleta's piano as the focus of the band.

'Coming across Oleta made me realise that soul music was the most direct way of being expressive: it was a musical form that a lot of people would readily recognise. It is a very common language. But we haven't tried to write soul songs on the album. We couldn't write tracks songs, because we are Tears For Fears and our songs have the lyrics of Tears For Fears songs. What we have tried to incorporate is the fluidity of expression that is found in great soul songs.'

Nicky: 'The song went through a number of changes before its final birth. Oleta's vocal and the gospel arrangement of the song provided the focus. Prior to that, there had been a number of versions, each one with a different slant. There was a version that leaned towards a Barry White feel, one that leaned towards Little Feat and one which leaned towards Steely Dan. We wrote a large part of it on the road in 1985, after Roland had heard various members of the crew maligning him late one night in the hotel room next door. The next day at the soundcheck, he sang the chorus and I started adding chords to it.

'From that day on, we played it at each soundcheck and new bits evolved as we went along. Similarly, the song continued to grow as it was recorded, first produced by Clive Langer and Alan Winstanley, then by Chris Hughes and finally by Tears For Fears with Dave Bascombe. Oleta was the key.'

Oleta: 'We had to play "Badman's Song" over and over before we finished it. Roland was on the point of exasperation because we had tried so many different ways, but it wasn't coming together. It finally gelled as a result of a jam session. Pino Palladino and Manu Katche started playing and I joined in and suddenly we had the song.'

badman's song

words and music by Orzabal / Holland

Piano solo

Heard ev-ery word that was said that night when the light of the world put the

world to right._____ Well here's to the boys back in

six two__ eight when an ear to the wall was a twist of fate._____

I will shine a blind-ing light through those hearts as black as night. Sticks and stones may break my bones, but at

least__ the seeds of love____ will be sown. 1. Now

once in a while when I feel no shame, I get down on my knees and I pray for rain__ and though the

(2.) guilt in the frame of the look-ing - glass_ puts a shine on the mind where re - flec-tions pass_ where the jig -

breeze blows gent-ly while I state my case,— there'll be cer-tain men wait-ing just to scratch my face.—
-saw pie-ces of a bro-ken man try and fit them-selves to-ge-ther a-gain—

Hand on my heart, I will make a stand for the life and the times of the
lies in dis-guise in the name of trust put your head in the sand it will

Mir-ror - man.—
turn to dust—— what's your problem? what's your curse? won't it make the mat - ter worse?

Chorus
In my head— there is a mir - ror when I've been bad,— I've been wrong.—

Food for the saints— that are quick to— judge— me, hope for the bad - man. This is the bad - man's song.

Instr.

2. Well 'They say

faith can move moun - tains, fire can cleanse your soul.' Faith can move moun - tains,— but

25

mind o - ver mat-ter won't stop all your chat-ter no!_____ Faith can move moun-tains.

Faith can move moun - tains, but mind o - ver mat-ter won't stop all your chat-ter no!

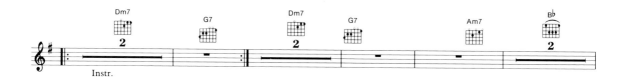

Instr.

Piano solo

VERSE 3:
I heard every word that was said last night
When the light of the world put the world to right
When I hear soft whispers at the break of day
(I'm in trouble every step of the way)
Sweet talking boys who can do no wrong
When the stories are tall as the day is long
With such a thin line drawn between friend and foe
Lord help me now and bless my soul!

Look at yourself – See how you lie
Your hands start shaking and you don't know why
Look at yourself – See how you lie
Your hands start shaking and you don't know why

CHORUS:
Well there's food for the saints that are quick to judge me
Hope for a Badman . . .

Roland: 'The initial idea for the song came from a programme on the radio about a guy who was putting together a collection of traditional English folk songs. He wasn't interested in the really common ones that appeared in songbooks, but in the lesser-known ones that had been passed down from generation to generation by word of mouth.

'The most interesting song he came across was called "The Seeds Of Love", which he had heard about from a gardener by the name of Mr England! It all seemed too good to be true – Mr England sowing the seeds of love! That gave me the title for the song.

'It is undoubtedly the most directly political song that Tears For Fears have ever recorded. In a way, that is not surprising, because it was written in the week of the 1987 General Election. Up to that point, I had never been very interested in politics. Being interested in psychology, I had always thought that everything began and ended with the individual. I used to dismiss the entire realm of politics as irrelevant, a pretty stupid viewpoint.'

'The initial idea for the song came from a programme on the radio about a guy who was putting together a collection of traditional English folk songs.'

'So I decided to find out more about it and began reading up on the history of socialism. The more I found out about the struggle of the working class in Britain, the more angry I became. It stirred up a lot of strong feelings inside me and a lot of those came out in the lyrics of Seeds.

'At the time, it was a big discovery for me. It was like watching someone beating up your little brother. It related to me in a personal way. I was very much a child of the Welfare State, brought up on a council estate in the sixties. I felt the urge to write some sort of protest song, something that I'd never attempted before. But I didn't want it to be a negative song, brimful of resentment.

'There is obviously a lot of resentment in left-wing argument and a lot of it is fair enough, but it can come across as very negative. I didn't want to fall into that trap. I wanted a more creative response. It upset me that a lot of Tory doctrine is based simply on balancing the books, an obsession with good housekeeping. It's all based on a rather dull pragmatism.

'I wanted to write something more optimistic. Optimism is not always an unrealistic option, particularly when it is blended with creativity. But I don't look on Seeds as any sort of rallying cry. It was a synchronous event. It coincided with a distinct loosening-up of attitudes. This might sound a bit naive and idealistic, but I think it is a sign of the way that people's ideals are gradually changing. The prevailing mood is moving away from the "politics of greed" towards a more caring and optimistic attitude.

'As a piece of music, all the evocations of the sixties on Seeds are very deliberate. We used a lot of Beatles influences on purpose. The Beatles are still the archetypal pop group. It is almost as if they never existed, as if they were a fantasy.

'The chords in the chorus are also very cliched. They are in the key of C Major, which is the big, optimistic key. My voice is very distorted in parts of the song. Sometimes it sounds like John Lennon, sometimes it sounds like Bob Dylan singing "Subterranean Homesick Blues", sometimes it sounds like David Bowie. The vocal influences are all from that era, the sixties and early seventies.

'All those very obvious influences gave the song an air of familiarity and enabled us to use it as a vehicle for what we wanted to say.'

sowing the seeds of love

words and music by Orzabal / Smith

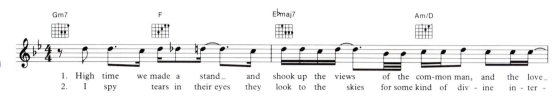

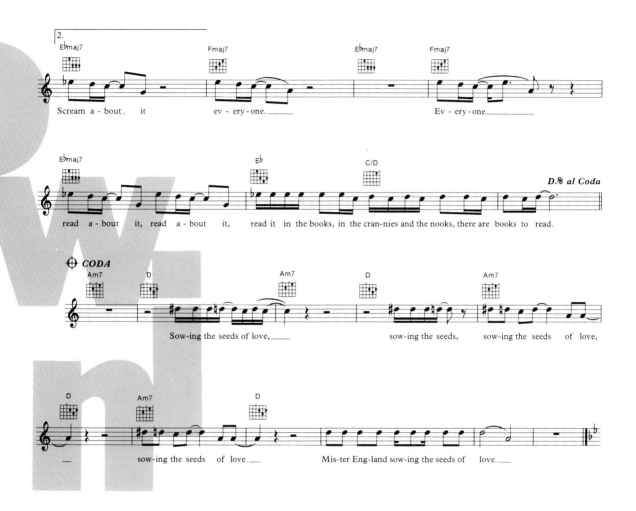

VERSE 3:
Time to eat all your words, swallow your pride, open your eyes.
High time we made a stand and shook up the view of the common man.
And the love train rides from coast to coast, every minute of every hour.
"I Love a Sunflower," and I believe in love power, Love Power, LOVE POWER!!!

CHORUS:
Sowing the Seeds
An end to need,
And the Politics of Greed
With Love.

Roland: 'It is a song about growing older, an acceptance of mortality. It's an acceptance of the fact that we do get older. It attempts to get in line with that. I have an incredible tendency always to look back, always to look inwards. That can be fine. But there also comes a point where I have to make things work in the present. There will always come a time when you have to bring yourself up to date.

'Too many people are living in a secret world. That line refers to people who are playing the roles of mothers and fathers – almost like in the playground – when they haven't really resolved their inner dilemma. It's a song about self-delusion, about people happy in the make-believe.

'You should always be evolving as a person if you are going to live life to the full. The same goes for a band if they are to remain relevant and creative. I watched a lot of music on TV while we were recording this album and so many of the records featured were by black hip-hop acts. It is another generation. The emphasis on youth and expression is brilliant. I love that music but, at the same time, I realise that it is not really me.'

'It is a song about growing older, an acceptance of mortality. It's an acceptance of the fact that we do get older. It attempts to get in line with that.'

'You should always be evolving within yourself. But you should also try to catch up with the age you are. There's no point in someone of 50 trying to compete with the youth that are into hip-hop. We do grow and evolve and we have to let go of certain things. We die as children and become adolescents. We die as adolescents and become adults. We have to let go of certain things. And sometimes it is very hard.'

Nicky: 'To get across the feelings of hope and despair involved with growing older, this song had to be approached with a wide-eyed innocence. The demo we recorded in 1986 at my flat in West Hampstead was the blueprint for the track. Whenever we went away from that initial feeling, the song no longer made any sense. I remember Roland playing me a mix of one of the versions of this song about a year and a half later. And I said to him "It sounds like we're already older." It was reflecting the time that had passed by and what was going on in the studio.

'About a year later we approached the song again, this time with Curt singing the lead vocal. It was the last track I worked on with them in the studio in April 1989 and the last track to be finished. It sounded fresh again. Curt's voice had all the emotional qualities that Roland's original possessed. It took a long time to recapture the innocence that had been lost.'

advice for the young at heart

words and music by Orzabal / Holland

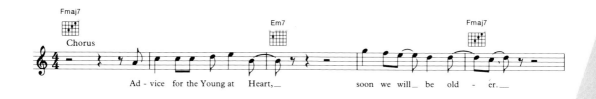

Chorus
Ad-vice for the Young at Heart,__ soon we will__ be old - er.

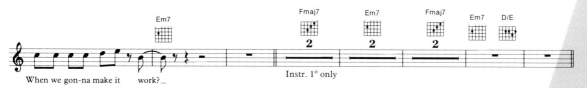

When we gon-na make it work?__   Instr. 1° only

1. Too ma-ny peo-ple__ liv-ing in a sec-ret__ world, while they__ play mo-thers and fa-thers,
2. Love is a pro-mise, love is a sou-ve - nir,__ once giv - en ne-ver for-got-ten,

we play lit - tle boys and__ girls.   When we gon-na make it   work?
ne-ver let it dis-ap - pear.   This could be__ our last__ chance

__   work - ing hour__ is o-   I could be hap - py, I could be quite nai - ve,__

it's on - ly me and my sha - dow hap-py in our make be - lieve.__ Soon,__

and with the hounds at bay,___ I'll call your bluff___
-ver.

'cause it would be o - kay___ to walk on tip - toes ev - er - y day. And when I
and how it makes me weep___ 'cause some-one sent___ my soul to___ sleep.

think of you and all the love that's due, I'll make a pro-mise, I'll___ make a stand___ 'cause to these

big brown eyes,___ this comes as no sur - prise. We've got the whole wide world___ in our hands.

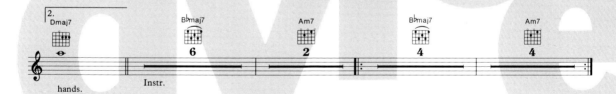

hands.   Instr.

CHORUS:
Advice for the Young at Heart
Soon we will be older
When we gonna make it work?
Working hour is over
We can do anything that we want
Anything that we feel like doing
Advice . . .

'The so-called civilised world always tries to solve Third World problems with First World solutions. We don't relate to the Third World in a very healthy way.'

'Roland: 'Like "Woman In Chains", this song can be taken on both a personal and a more global level. It is about the conflict and contrasts between a feeling of security and the threats of life's darker areas. It is about having one foot in the womb, happy in the sense of cosy containment, and one foot in the backroads and basements of our lives.

'The song starts with a feeling of being safely contained. I never slept so hard and never dreamt so well. It's about that beautiful feeling when the darker, barren things are all out of reach. It's much the same as the general attitude to the Third World. If it is out of sight, it is out of mind.

'The so-called civilised world always tries to solve Third World problems with First World solutions. We don't relate to the Third World in a very healthy way. We export food, but we don't export much enlightenment. The only education we give the Third World is lessons in consumerism. As the song says, hungry men will close their minds because ideas are not their food. On a different scale, the same principle applies to the greed that is prevalent in Britain as well.

'We took a lot of criticism for not doing Live Aid, but there was something that didn't feel right about it to me. Although we gave a multitude of excuses at the time, there was also the fact that I didn't *want* to do it. We did Sport Aid the year after, motivated partly by guilt over the Live Aid thing. But I was still very wary of compassion as a fashion. I do have a problem with that crowd mentality. I find something inherently dangerous in a crowd relying on external symbols — in this case pop stars — to tell them what is right and wrong.

'I know a lot of good came out of Live Aid, and a lot of money was raised, but I think people should be weaned off this dependency on a symbol. It is fine when it is a charity, but some time in the future it could just as easily be a different political movement with a different ideology. It is those circumstances that breed fascist movements. It is an abuse of the religious instinct. People have a desire to follow the crowd.'

standing on the corner of the third world

words and music by Orzabal

1. Man, I ne - ver slept___ so hard,	I
2. Fill their dreams with big___ fast car,
3. Hun - gry man will close___ their minds,	i -

ne - ver dreamt so well,___	dream - ing I was
fill their head___ with sand,___	ho - ly white, we'll
-deas are not___ their food,___	no - tions fall on

safe in life	like mus-sels in a shell.___	Roll - ing and con -
paint their town	the col - our of our flag.___	Hey there lit - tle
sto - ny ground	where pas-sions are sub - dued.___	Col - our all the

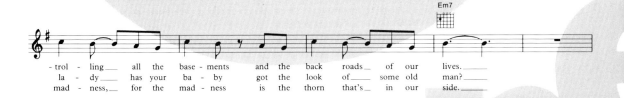

-trol - ling___ all the base - ments and the back roads___ of our lives.___
la - dy___ has your ba - by got the look of___ some old man?
mad - ness,___ for the mad - ness is the thorn that's___ in our side.___

Stand - ing on the cor - ner of the Third World.___

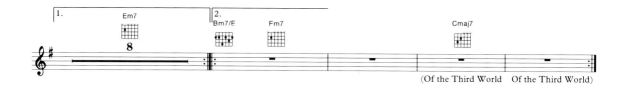

(Of the Third World   Of the Third World)

When we gon - na learn?___ Who we gon - na turn___ to?___ The pro - mis - es they make,

the call for our at - ten - tion,___ com - pas - sion___ is the fash - ion.

Free to earn, our poc - kets burn,___ we buy___ for love,___

die for love. _____

INSTR: +
Hold me I'm crying
Hold me I'm dying

Roland: 'The song was originally written for the Alex Cox film *Sid and Nancy*, but it was rejected by the makers because it was deemed not punk enough. In the end, I thought the film itself could have been better. It should have been shot as a proper movie rather than an attempted rockumentary.

'Nicky Holland gave me the book that Nancy Spungen's mother had written about her daughter and the relationship with Sid Vicious. The book is called *And I Don't Want To Live This Life*, and was about Nancy's life from the moment of birth onwards.'

'I do tend to feel that some people's lives are more fated than others. Some people really do not have much choice.'

'Nancy Spungen was born with the umbilical cord wrapped round her neck. Sher was also jaundiced and her blood type was incompatible with her mother's. Anything that could have gone wrong did go wrong. In the book, her mother draws the analogy between the needle marks in the heels of the newly born baby and the track marks on her teenage daughter from the injection of heroin.

'In the song, I then make another analogy with the knife that ended her life. Life begins with needles and pins, it ends with swords and knives. As a song, it is a lament.

'I do tend to feel that some people's lives are more fated than others. Some people really do not have much choice.'

Nicky: 'This song began as a piano piece, reminiscent of Eric Satie and Claud Debussy, etc. Roland thought it sounded like a film theme, a *leitmotif* that recurs throughout a picture in different shapes and sizes. We had both read Deborah Spungen's *And I Don't Want To Live This Life* and when we heard that Alex Cox was making a film of the story, we decided to put the two ideas together.

'It was the first song we had a finished demo of — the film company needed it — and when they rejected it, Tears For Fears said that they would record it. The song grew a bit more in the studio — Chris Hughes wanted to open the middle section out and suggested that we wrote about 64 bars of music before the final theme returned! So we wrote a frame for this departure section and started layering things on top of it.'

swords and knives

words and music by Orzabal / Holland

Intro.

1. A - wak - ing world of in - no - cence,___ so

2. Oh dan - ger - man, oh dan - ger - man,___ your

grave those first born cries._____ When life be-gins____ with need-les and pins,___ it

blade fits like a glove._____ When forged in steel____ time can-not heal_____ that

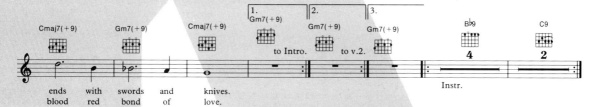

to Intro.   to v.2.

ends with swords and knives.

blood red bond of love.

Instr.

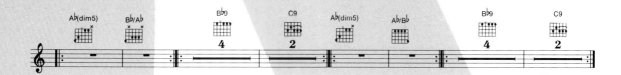

Turn the ta - bles, we'll burn the fa - bles   lies be-neath the vis-ions and day-dreams

fooled by now, we my-sti-fy __ the past ____ like a dream, like it ne-ver hap-pened.

VERSE 3: (Instr.) +
In times of trouble you're an open book
With the change in the way you look
And it's sad love's not enough
To make things better

VERSE 4:
When life begins with needles and pins
It ends with Swords and Knives
God save those born to die

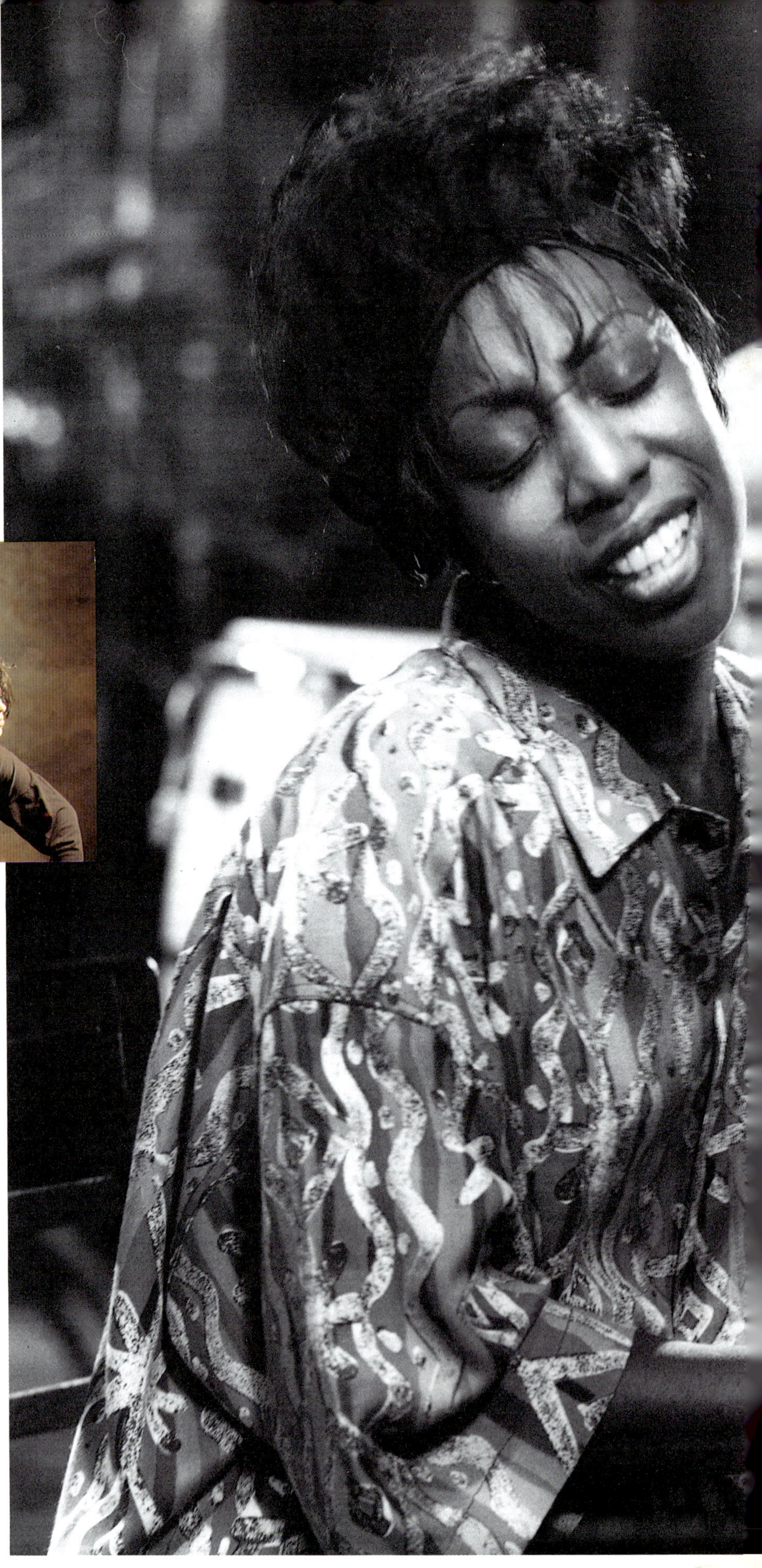

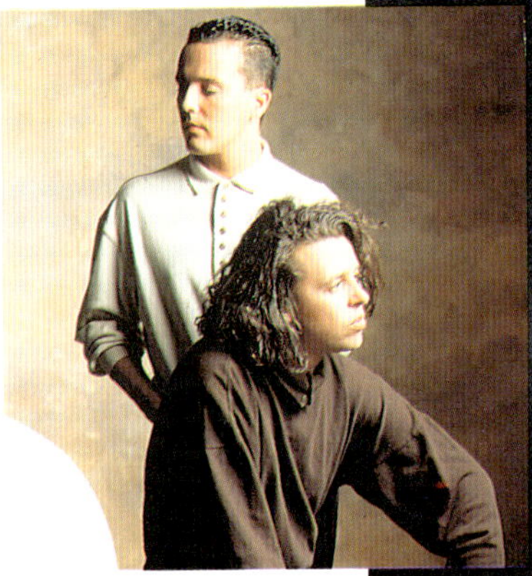

Roland: 'The imagery on "Year Of The Knife" is very different from the imagery on "Swords And Knives". Here it is the knife that separates, the knife that cuts the attachment between two people. It signifies the death of a relationship, the parting of two people who are very close.

'It is one of the most aggressive songs on the album, one of the most aggressive songs we have ever recorded. It is strange, because the aggression is not contrived or deliberate, but it was obviously there when we were recording the album. "Year Of The Knife" has four guitar parts in it. The lead part is played by Robbie McIntosh, but there are also guitars played by Randy Jacob of Was (Not Was), Neil Taylor and myself.

'The song itself is very gutsy. At the time of recording, I wanted to hear something that was as gutsy as I felt. I didn't want to hear an *approximation* of the way I felt. I wanted something real.

'This might sound a strange thing to say about an album that took so long to record, but this track is actually a bit rough in places.'

Nicky: 'One afternoon I went round to Roland's house and he played me a new idea he had come up with entitled "Too Late For The Young Gun". Neil Taylor, the guitarist, was round there too and the three of us started playing around with the idea. Neil was playing a great rhythm part and I was accidently marking each measure with the beat in the wrong place. This created rhythmic tension and the song just sort of spontaneously happened as a result. Once that was there, everything else started to fall into place and the song became titled "Year Of The Knife".'

'It is one of the most aggressive songs on the album, one of the most aggressive songs we have ever recorded.'

year of the knife

words and music by Orzabal / Holland

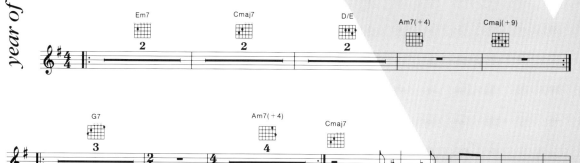

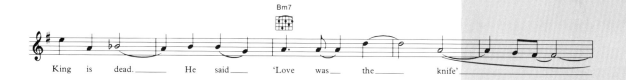

Hal - le - lu - jah the

King is dead. He said 'Love was the knife'

and now he'll dream some magic queen might try, might try and

save his life. They say his fam - ous

fin - al words came from the heart of the man.

He made his bed on love den - ied, he played Jek-yll and Hyde 'til the
I made my bed on love den - ied, now I ain't gon-na

day he died.
sleep to - night.

Chorus
Oh, too late for the young gun to lead a sim - ple life.

Too late for the young gun.

This is this is the year of the knife,

this is the year of the knife.

See the moun - tains crum - ble, feel the fire go cold,

Repeat Chorus
then *D.*𝄌

sum - mer will turn to win - ter, love will turn to stone.

'The mood of this song is very tranquil — two people completely resigned to the fact that they are going to die.'

Roland: 'The song is about the acceptance of mortality again. There is a line that begins "I will decay". People do decay, but it shouldn't be a problem. Death is still a taboo subject. It remains the unthinkable and the unmentionable. There are still all these black and dark images that go with it.

'But I think there is another level to take it on, an awareness of how we fit into the chain of life, the family chain. We are not immortal. But in some senses there is still life after a death. There is the cycle of life and death. Everyone keeps something of their parents inside them, for instance, even if one or both of those parents are dead. It's a simple song, but I like it a lot. It's a sad, melancholic note and a good one to end the album on.

'There is a snippet of the spoken word at the beginning of the track: "Let's take five minutes." That's just a bit of fun. It's a bit of studio chat that somehow made it onto the tape. The idea is that the album took a bit more than five minutes to complete… We thought it would take a much shorter period of time when we began recording… famous last words.'

Nicky: 'This song was originally titled "The 17 Year Locust". The mood of this song is very tranquil — two people completely resigned to the fact that they are going to die. I feel it is this stillness that gives the song its potency. It's one of my favourites on the album. Most of the music came first, except for the middle section, which provides a release from the tension set up by the lyric.

'Roland always wanted someone else to sing the verses, Tom Waits in particular or maybe Robbie Robertson, but I love the way he does it. There's a real strength in vulnerability.'

Roland: 'At one stage I wanted to call the album 'Famous Last Words.' I really liked the title of an Elvis Costello album, *Goodbye Cruel World,* and it was designed as a vague echo of that. It has a note of finality. It is a good note to end on.

'It may yet turn out to be our last album.'

famous last words

words and music by Orzabal / Holland

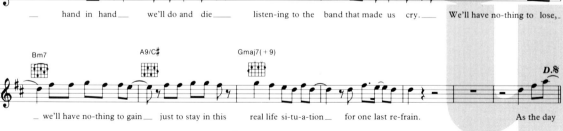

1. Af-ter the wash,___ be-fore the fire___
2. 'A' for a heart,___ 'B' for a brain___

I will de-cay,___ melt in your arms.___ As the day___ hits the night___ we will sit___
in-sects and grass___ are all that remain. When the light___ from a-bove___ burns a hole

___ by can-dle-light,___ we will laugh,___ we will sing___ 'When the saints go march-ing in'
___ straight through our love,___

in' and we will car-ry war. All our love___

and all of our pain___ will be but a tune,___ the sun and the moon___ the wind and the rain,___

___ hand in hand___ we'll do and die___ listen-ing to the band that made us cry.___ We'll have no-thing to lose,___

___ we'll have no-thing to gain___ just to stay in this real life si-tu-a-tion___ for one last re-frain. As the day

'It has a note of finality. It is a good note to end on. It may yet turn out to be our last album

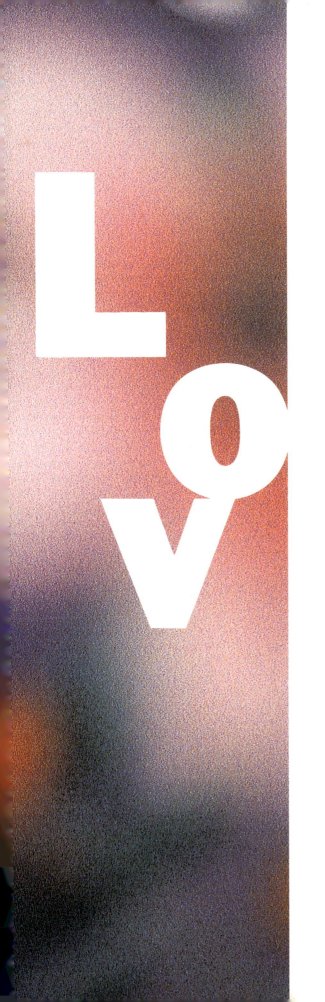